This Is How You Love Her

Cassandra Alfred

Dedication:

To My Younger Self.
And to all the women, women in transition, and girls out there
learning to love themselves.

Preface

When I was a child I used to cry out,
"This is so hard."
I would think,
No one teaches you how to do this:
How to live life.
There's no rule book,
No comprehensive guide on:

How to make friends.
How to handle losing them.
How to fall in love with the right person.
How to learn who the right person is.
How to learn who the right person is not.
How to love yourself in a society that gives you every reason not to.
How to have hope in the face of adversity.
How to be strong.
How to be okay with being weak.

After trials and tribulations,
So many highs and so many lows,
I realized that no, we are not given a guide book on how to live life.
The reason?
We are meant to write our own.

thoughts on life

Perhaps I began scribbling the first lines of this book on the slate of my unconscious.

...

Marita Golde

Dear Reader,

Maybe these words won't mean much to you.
Maybe you won't be able to see the heart hidden between the
pages.
Maybe you won't see the womyn who wants this to matter.

Sincerely,

Doubt.

Take whatever hurts you have,

Lay them among these pages.

Tucked into the margins,

Your secrets are safe.

Unconditional

Love self.

Raw self.

Hurt self.

Charred self.

No matter.

Love self.

All self.

Womyn,

God stitched life into the lining of our wombs.

Born from the body with the ability to form a body,

We are the physical manifestation of infinity.

Yet the presence of a womb means death for us.

Irony.

How many girls have died after taking their first breaths?

Valued less because they would grow up to be

Womyn.

Who would think that the sticky red blood that falls from the juncture between our thighs could mean disgust.

Womyn.

Burned. Mutilated. Raped.

These are our headlines.

Womyn.

God stitched life into the lining of our wombs,

A miracle.

How can we be so overlooked?

I used to live life with my heart wide open.

I have since learned to keep it closed.

I have always been a hornet's nest
I have always been cracked glass

easily broken
easily shattered

I don't want to be steel
I don't want to be fortress

I have a heart as open as an ocean
I have created rivers with my tears

easily moved
easily injured

I don't want to be ice
I don't want to be marble

Should I be fire?
Should I burn?

I am tired of tasting ash in my mouth
I am tired of cupping bruises on my cheek

I don't want to be brick
I don't want to be concrete

Can I be some of one and not too much of the other?

There is lot of pain and loss in trying to learn

both ways of being

I have learned to grow thorns.

Yet, I am trying not to lose the tender parts of me.

People tell me to be confident,
I tell them confidence is learned.
When I was a kid I thought confidence
was a blond-haired, blue-eyed girl.

A Poem Cut Too Short

I'm tired of people telling me that
Those men, kids, fathers, sons,
Wouldn't have died if they'd just stop resisting.
As if there wasn't a human in that black body.
As if there wasn't a heart inside that black body.
As if there wasn't a soul inside that black body.

As if -

Sometimes people want to destroy beautiful souls because
That's easier than watching them shine.

Clearly

Daughter, one day you'll be at your wits' end.
Eyebrows furrowed, arms crossed,
I'll have vexed you for some reason.
I'll have made you scowl or cry.
You'll ask me, "Don't you love me?"
I'll say:

Daughter, I love you.

Clearly, I do.

I am a textbook of mistakes and lessons,
Pages upon pages of scribbled out sentences.
Red marks with red pen,

Edits and edits and edits again.

Do not look at me and intend to find perfection.
You are the only example of perfection I claim.
I may be unfair.
I may act like I know more than I do.

But

Do I love you?

Clearly, I do.

All that's left is the best of myself,

And I give it all to you.

I used to shrink myself.
Making myself smaller,
I felt like I took up too much

s   p   a   c   e

I was aware of my
Expanding waist.
A plus sign among minuses,
Higher and wider than my classmates,
The only way to silence my loud body was to be quiet.
I learned to exist just below the surface,
Learned how to divert attention.

I grew up wanting to lose parts of myself.
I got used to curling inwardly.

The challenge came in learning how to unfurl,
Release.
Doing away with maladaptive ways of adapting,
I unfolded and smoothed out the wrinkles in the sheet.
Slowly.

I realized that I deserve to be here.

It's okay to take up all this

s   p   a   c   e

14

One day, I will look at myself in the mirror and not wish to see someone else.

Remember, you are a garden.
Soft dirt.
Tread lightly upon yourself.

Gardens need consistency and tender hands.
Remove weeds that threaten to suffocate you.

Those around you are the gardeners.
Keep only those that help you flourish.
Fire the rest.

Nothing in life stays the same.
You'll change along with the seasons.
One flower dies and another takes its place.

It's okay to build a fence around your garden.
Just don't forget to build a gate.

the world
will try
to break
you.
stay whole.

you will fall in and out of love with life many times but still

— keep living.

The brightest smiles often mask the deepest of pains
(1-800-273-8255).

Icarus

It's not easy to move mountains,
It's not easy to redirect streams.

It's not easy to grow gardens.
Weeds grow faster than you think.

How can we stare down the mouth of a lion?
How can we beat the devil back?

But alas,

Alas,

We try to catch sunlight in the palm of our hands.

In the palm of our hands.

We try to catch sunlight.

Perhaps we get singed.

Maybe we fall.

Or we land.

thoughts on love

I am deathly afraid of heartbreak and disappointment, and letting people in comes with the very real risk of both.

...

Shalon Irving

It is sometimes dangerous

to want love.

if
you
knew
the
kind
of
love
that
made
you,

you
wouldn't
settle
for
anything
less

Rorschach

Can I be measured?
What ruler should I lay my body against?
Can a ruler ever measure the true depths of a vessel?
Can you?
I have gifts hidden inside my mind.
Look closely and see the sunrise on the surface of my eyes.

Cut me open, spill my blood, like ink on paper.
Tell me what you see.
Does it frighten you?
Does it make you uneasy?
Good.
I do not exist to blanket you against the world.

My skin carries marks - hills and grooves.
Will you be able to read me?
Will I boggle your mind?
Am I too much a challenge?
Am I too difficult a climb?

Am I a battlefield worth crossing,
Despite the cannon fire?

love me in rough waters,
not just calm seas.

i love. i love. i love.

too much.

Healing takes place on tear soaked pillow cases and wrinkled bed sheets.

During those quivering hours after midnight, before dawn.
Pitch darkness or brilliant light.
Healing happens during triumph and during defeat.
Among family, friends , lovers and pets.

Healing is: Music. Nature. Poetry. Coffee. Tea. Dancing. Art.

A recipe for loving yourself.

A Dead Rose

My love for you is a dead rose.
Preserved. Dried. Set aside.
Curled petals attached to a withered stem.
The colors faded to a dusky red.
No longer vibrant and alive, but brittle and dead.

However, the beauty remains the same way it was then.

I wish that we had met each other now that we are whole.
But would we have become whole if we had not met each other
When we were broken?

Fists. Knives. Flames.

I stood face to face with the worst of myself.
Kissing my palm,
I touched my hand to her face.
I whispered, "I love you still."

We stepped into one another.

I became whole.

hurt me now
so I don't get hurt
later.

Does it feel good to wrap yourself in his "Babys?"
Blanket yourself with hollow words,
Promises that break too easy?
You are thrilled at the briefest moments,
The kisses and caresses that drive you.
They never satisfy you,
Your heart still feels uneasy.
You cling to him and memorize the feel of his arms around you.
Does it warm you when you're cold at night and alone?
How long can you swim in his apologies,
Before you drown.
The
      "I'll do better next time."
      "Nobody taught me how to love."
      "Nobody understands me like you."
Can you continue ignoring the woman that needs you as much as
you need him.
Don't you see her in your eyes when you're staring at your phone
screen?
      He said, "I'll call."
Or when you're staring at the bathroom mirror, tears in your eyes.
      He said, "This time, for real."
When will you realize there ain't no making people love you?
Love yourself.
      People will come.

By losing you, I found the greatest of loves.
It was in myself.
Thank you.

Be careful loving people who paint futures without you in it.

You tell me to hit you up when I'm in your city.
Is that code for you miss me?
Or code for you'd like to see me but it's okay if you don't?
I've never been good with reading between the lines.
In my eyes it's either you do or you don't.,
You will or you won't.
I've never been one for that wishey-washy,
Timey-wimey,
Maybe,
Sorta
Kinda shit.
Let's be Facebook friends, not really friends kinda shit.
The "I'd love to see you again,"
Can't commit to a plan kinda shit.
Just be honest and cut the shit.
You're attracted by what you see but that's just not enough.
I'm a big girl. I can handle that.
But don't confuse my fat for a punching bag.
I am not an option.
I don't need your indecision.
I know my worth.
I see right through you.
So if you have a problem making decisions that's fine.
You are not going to waste my time.

Sometimes you don't get closure.
You just have to move on.

Negro Sunshine

Negro Sunshine
I am the light they thought would die in the casket.
I am the music that could not be silenced,
The scream they tried to quell with their fingers and nooses.

Negro sunshine.
Silk forged from fire.
Ship that sailed despite the storm.
Light that pierced mist and rain and fog.

Negro sunshine.
Strange fruit you could not hang.
The beauty you failed to recognize.
The glory you tried to destroy.
I am negro sunshine.

Black. Radiant.
Spilling joy.
Sunshine.

I am. They are.
He is. She is.

I am. They are.
He is. She is

thoughts on self

At a certain point in your life, probably when too much of it has gone by, you will open your eyes and see yourself for who you are...especially for everything that made you so different from all the awful normals. And you will say to yourself, 'But I am this person.' And in that statement, that correction, there will be a kind of love.

...

Phoebe in Wonderland

If you've got compliments followed by an "If Only," then you can keep them.
I don't want to hear your review on how I can improve my figure,
'Cause I figure you mean well but your constructive criticism falls short.

Pretty if...

Attractive if...

Could you just...

It only serves to construct me into a product of your wishes.
You size me up and consider that I can round down a few pounds.
Curl it. Nip it. Perm it. Trim it.

Well maybe I should.

But I've got enough closets full of
"If Onlys," & *"If You Just Coulds".*

Like a road shrouded by fog.
Your kind mentioning and deliberations leave me with a gloomy forecast.
Setting up an elusive dream of:

What I Can Be Vs. The Present Me

And for some reason the present me always seems to lose.

I understand the need for beauty but is that the only outcome?
Is that the only way the fight of life is won?
Now there's nothing wrong with taking pride in your looks or being well groomed,
But why is that society's main role and I always fail to make the call backs?
Is it so hard to see my marvelous soul hidden beneath fat pads and skin folds?

I'm sorry if my body doesn't soothe you.
But do you love me for me for love me for you?
I was raised on the right hand of the Father
And He said, and I quote, that
"Love is not self- seeking."
If I was made in His likeness, can you not believe that I am one of
God's finest?

I admit that there was a time where I didn't think like this.
I was blinded.
Thinking that the more mass I retained the less from life I deserved
to obtain,
Constantly on a quest for perfection that left me parched…and
hungry.
Spiritually dissatisfied
That's what happens when you're conditioned to believe that self-
acceptance depends on conditions
If only you could realize that my qualities and personality surpass
my clothing size.
Not even the stepping scale could measure the weight of my
endless love.
For those who do not take the time to discover the unknown
treasure troves of my golden soul they'll forever
Measure me against a ruler labeled in:

Pretty if…

Attractive if…

Couldn't you just…

"If Only."

On my knees and out of luck I decided to look inward, and not
outward.
I found God in myself and I loved her fiercely
I dared to love,
All of me.
Even the parts I find most hard to love.

I'll love myself hard enough to make up for every wound, filled with self-doubt and hurt,

I'll do it alone

If by myself

If I,

Only.

Untitled

I wonder if the flower cries when we pick it?

I wonder why, when we see beautiful things,

We must make it our own?

I wonder, if we saw the flower cry, would we leave it alone?

Pardon the noise.
I am currently under

c
O
n
s
T
R

U
c
t

I
O
N

A work in progress.
Due date to be determined.

I apologize in advance for the falling debris,
I am a masterpiece in the making.

It is okay to be soft.

Do not let the world make you crumble.

I cannot hide myself to please other people.
To do that is to cast myself in shadow.
I deserve to be in the light.

Mine

It may be
Bruised.
Battered.
Bloodied.
Scarred.

But it's mine.

It may have bullied.
Marked.
Cursed.

But it's mine.

It may have been doused in flames.
Laid to waste.

But it's mine.

This.

This.

This is mine.

Sometimes I am pink,
I am sunrise and sunsets.
Other days I am green.
Tall.
Oak.
Branches.
Reaching.
Lush. Vegetation. Life.

I am yellow,
Lion's mane.
Mighty.
Mighty.
I roar.

Yet sometimes I am blue.
I am rainfall on window panes,
Streaking.
Other days I am gray,
Cast over cloudy skies.
Red,
Heart bleeding. Exposed. Beating.

I am a rainbow.
Pretty,
Captivating.

Dripping paint down a canvas,
Messy.
Abstract.

He said he doesn't like all those options,
Variations, combinations, shades, and hues.
He wants someone easily digestible, practical.
Someone to hang over the mantelpiece.
More refined.
Easier to define.
I'm sorry if I can't fit into your crayon box.
In there I don't breathe too easy.
I can't stay inside your black lines,
Your prison.
You can't see the masterpiece inside.
Yes, I am not easy but this rainbow is enuf.

This rainbow.

Pretty.
Captivating.
Dripping paint down a canvas.
Messy.
Abstract.

I am a rainbow.

I am.

All these.

And much more

Some days I love my body a lot.
Some days I love my body a little.

Of course you're scarred.

You spent years battling yourself.
No one leaves a war unwounded.

My Sad

My sad.
It is a welcome home I have grown to know well.

The dark figure at the corner of my eye.
I thought I'd out ran it.

My sad sits in the back of my car while I'm driving.
I can't see the headlights.

My sad keeps me company.
Its whispers keep me up at night.

My oldest friend.
I don't know how I would sleep without it.

Get help?
I won't know what to do with myself when my sad is gone.

It has always been a part of me.
Losing it may be like losing me.

Do I need more help than I think.?

I tell people I am tired. It is easier than saying,
"This morning, I had trouble getting out of bed."

Devil,
You cannot live here - within me.
There is no room for you here.

Muted Color

Sometimes I feel like muted color,

    Newspaper lying too long in the sun.

Like dull greens and pale yellows.
Bricks weathered by rain,
Browns covered in dust.
If one were to point to a painting and ask,
"Who are you?"
I'd point to the background blues.

I am peeling layers and old paint.
"Put another coat on," they say,
"You're beginning to fade."

I don't wanna be mute.
I want to be the fire-engine red racing down the tar,
Eye catching and radiant.

I want to shine!

I'm tired of not being bright enough
To catch someone's eye.
I want to be the first picked from the crayon box,
The last put back.
I want to be inside that black outline...

    Me.

But instead, I'm deaf, blind, and dumb.

I feel like muted color,

    Newspaper lying too long in the sun.

Do not feel guilty about seeking out your own happiness.

Skin Like Wings

I don't know why I was born with such thin skin.
Skin like tissue paper.
Butterfly wings.
Skin that absorb so much.
Sad faces, furrowed brows, and cold silences.

Somehow I had a way of absorbing the world.

Never knowing how to let it out.

Not knowing how to soothe the storm clouds
I carried it all.
I became so heavy.
I thought it was my warrant.
My duty.
The storm would gather, grow, and thunder –
Symphonies between my ears.
Torrents of rain pooled in my eyes and fell.
Doomed to live so heavy.

Until I learned how to release.

I still have butterfly wings,
Translucent and thin.
My skin gleams magnificently now,
Colors vibrant in the glow of the sun
Or the ray of the moon.

I used to live life with my heart closed.

I have learned to open it up to the right people.

I am one part sweetness.

One part sadness.

To The Unpicked Flower

You feel overlooked.
Disrespected.
Misunderstood.
It is okay to be the unpicked flower.
You get to bloom.

Your petals will multiply,
Your stalk will grow tall and firm.
You will reach for the sun.

You will be breathtaking.

Things to Remember::

1. You have always been enough.

2. You can't force someone to make you a priority.

3. Allow yourself to be loved.

4. This person (who you are now) is okay.

5. Be your best relationship.

You want to know how to love her?
Unlearn.
Unlearn the chiding, the distasteful commentary of others.
Unlearn the years of self-doubt and self-loathing,
Unlearn the lies you told yourself.
Unlearn it all.

Or at least try.

Remember,
Though we are cut down,
We grow back twice as tall.

Untitled

The snow tastes like salt.
A Little Red Boat fills with water and tips over.
I am like that.
I fill with water and tip over.
But I rescue myself.
I straighten myself out.
I continue to float on the water.

end

from the author

I truly believe art heals.
It healed me.

acknowledgements

Thank you to the support of my wonderful family and friends for their never ending support.
Thanks to Rockland Poets for helping me find my voice.

Credit goes to Sergio Jimenez for his work as editor.
Round of applause to Bandon M. Avant of Rtistic ART along with Toni & Alisha of Statement Goods Design for contributing to my cover art.

To all my readers:
May this have been more than a book to you.
May it have been a journey.

See:
www.thewomynwhowrites.com
Contact:
thewomynwhowrites@outlook.com
Follow:
@TheWomynWhoWrites

Made in the USA
Middletown, DE
24 November 2021